MW01143183

ALSO BY MATTHEW D. HUTCHESON

SEASONS

DAILY INSPIRATION FOR EVERY SEASON OF LIFE

Matthew D. Hutcheson
Annette Hutcheson

Edited by Kirsten Swenson Martineau

MACH 6
P R E S S™

This book resides in the following BISAC categories:

Body, Mind & Spirit / Inspiration & Personal Growth
Self-Help / Personal Growth / Happiness

BelloHutch

For more about Matthew D. Hutcheson and
other writings, visit www.bellohutch.com

In Latin, *bello* means "fight for."
BelloHutch@gmail.com

Mach 6 Press
mach6llc@gmail.com

Edited by Kirsten Swenson Martineau

ISBN: 978-1-365-90729-6

Printed in the United States of America

Dedication

For all the families still waiting.

January 1

Believe in yourself
because you should.
If you truly knew yourself,
you would!

January 2

I stared fear down
and what did I see?
Terror in its eyes . . .
Fear was afraid of me.

January 3

There is one particular reoccurring thing about life, the exhilarating effects of which I shall never tire. It is that special moment when reality prevails over perception and all 'superficial appearances' that had predominated up to that point vanish, revealing the splendor of what actually 'is.' Otherwise, I would be permanently misinformed or misled about that truly beautiful and magnificent something or someone.

January 4

Somehow the entire world
seems to have forgotten that
IT'S OK TO BE
H A P P Y!

January 5

Wisdom is the ability to see the
consequence of an action not yet taken.

Wisdom is the ability to refrain from
interfering when someone you love is about
to make a decision he or she will most
certainly regret.

Wisdom, also, is knowing what to
say, if and when to speak, and
to not make things worse if
you must speak or intervene.

January 6

When you become aware of
what you do not know, what you
need to know, and what you
want to know, let me know.

The secret of success
is easy to express.
To fail, and fail,
and fail again,
. . . only less, and less,
and less.

January 8

Do all you agree to do,
do not encroach,
Always be true, and
easy to approach.

January 9

Hope is your air.
Keep breathing it in.

January 10

Making your bed is not about sheets,
Nor is doing the dishes about plates.
Neither are, in and of themselves,
amazing feats.
Yet each is consistently done by
humanity's greats.

January 11

You can have what you want,
just not 'that way.'
Don't feel daunt, just
find a better way.

January 12

'Doing' is important for happiness;
Even more importantly 'gratitude.'
For the privilege 'to do' is the
universal key to the master lock.

January 13

Fear yields to curiosity, and
Dread yields to anticipation.

January 14

Brush your teeth and tongue when you are told, and you will have teeth when you are old. If you start early in your youth, you will retain more than just one tooth. Brushing twice is doubly nice and worthwhile for breath and smile.

January 15

Learn to communicate with your eyes.
People prefer to listen to kind eyes.
It's true for both gals and guys.
Never belittle because it's being 'little.'

January 16

Asking yourself, 'How valuable am I?' will only discourage you. The more elevating question is, 'Am I valuable to someone?'

January 17

Your life feels out of control because you have not controlled your thoughts. So all you know is 'feeling,' which keeps you 'reeling.' You can get control by disciplining your thoughts and acting the way you ought.

January 18

Every single choice is followed by a consequence, without exception.

January 19

I hope your heart hears this: You don't have to be disappointed in yourself anymore. A little disappointment now and then is good as a motivator for improvement and to try again. But if disappointment has become more than that, it has gone too far.

January 20

Every person is imbued with something special from God. Its manifestation comes so subtly and so naturally that many people miss it, until one day it dawns on them . . . 'Oh, it has been here all along.'

January 21

Most people silently believe their lives are meaningless. They would be stunned to see just how favorably consequential their lives actually are, even to people they don't know.

January 22

Beautiful is what you choose to be.

January 23

There are other places to live, you know?
There are other ways to go, you know?
There are other things to do, you know?
There are many, not few, you know?
There are other ways to grow, you know?

January 24

Regrets can often be averted
if you remember that the
better decision
may be inverted.

January 25

You have full control over what will and what will not become your life's regrets.

January 26

A shortcut is a short sell. Do not cut or sell yourself short because it is easier. Do not cheat yourself or your life of better experiences and outcomes. Self-respect and satisfaction in life is directly tied to choosing the more difficult yet correct paths. Disappointment and loss of self-respect is directly tied to choosing the more convenient yet incorrect paths. Every ordinary human being knows which path is which. Most choose the latter and then blame others for the outcomes of their poor choices. Do not do that. Show a little wisdom in yourself and pride in your potential. Have a little self-respect now so you may enjoy a lot of self-respect later.

January 27

"No (one) was ever wise by chance."
    –Seneca

January 28

It may not matter,
or it might.
Because of the latter,
do what is right.

January 29

Making your bed will get
Yesterday out of your head.

January 30

Do one thing well,
make it sing,
make it swell.

January 31

Speak graciously even
when treated audaciously.
The key to enduring is
anticipation and curiosity!

February 1

There is beauty within you that
only words can express.

February 2

What words you choose is less important than what tone you use.

February 3

Of all the things within your power to
change your life today and cause
dividends to be paid tomorrow
is to speak in a benevolent tone.

February 4

Benevolent means
well-meaning and kind.
Benevolent is formed from two Latin
words, 'bene,' which means 'well,' and
'velle,' which means 'wish.' Together
forming 'wellwish.'

February 5

Kindness is king.
Honesty is kind.
Humility is kind.

February 6

'How am I doing?'
'I love you.'
'I am sorry.'
'I made a mistake.'
Those are simple
responses that heal.

February 7

Sincerely wrap every word
in a benevolent tone and
watch how your life
changes for the better.

February 8

Do you need to say it?
Really?
Will it nourish, encourage, and strengthen?
Start asking yourself this
question before you speak.

February 9

Be soft as soapstone in expressing
thoughts towards her, and hard as
graphene in protecting her,
especially her feelings.

February 10

'We often refuse to accept
an idea merely because
the tone of voice in which it has been
expressed is unsympathetic to us.'
–Friedrich Nietzsche

February 11

The response of a listener, warm or
cold, favorable or resistant, is
activated based on the presence or
absence of benevolence
in the tone of the speaker.

February 12

To understand poetry, one must
drown in each individual word.

February 13

Don't try to impress her. Just let her know she makes you happy and show your authentic happiness in your face and tone in your voice.

February 14

Passion is chemistry that usually
diminishes over time. Love is the work of
empathy and respect that increases over
time. In the end, empathy and respect
remain and are the evidence of love.

February 15

There is nothing more
beautiful and desirable
than to faithfully
grow old together.

February 16

What will she remember about you? Let
it bring tears of happiness to her eyes.

February 17

Waste no more time
talking about what a
good man is like.
Be one.
—Marcus Aurelius

Obey society's common manners and
use language's proper grammars.

February 19

Men, forgive quickly,
And ask for
forgiveness even faster!
Don't argue; you
will not outlast her!

February 20

Differences teach us tolerance, test preconceived notions, and expand our horizons. Like great art or a beautiful garden, the whole is enhanced by accents and complementary colors and interesting shapes.

February 21
___

Today, touch your burning wick to
the extinguished wick of another.

February 22

Never respond at first reading or hearing if
you feel a reaction from it. Just don't
respond today. Perhaps respond
tomorrow, but not necessarily.
Perhaps do not respond at all.
Wise people never respond in the
moment. Foolish people always do.

February 23

Decisions made exclusively from
emotions eventually create an
environment of chaos.

February 24

Live life at your own pace.
Living life is not a race.

February 25

To wish someone well is to be
benevolent towards them.

February 26

Be not weary in well doing.

February 27

Very few things help a person succeed
in life more than a benevolent tone.

February 28

True benevolence is void of pretense or pretext. True benevolence of tone carries messages, even very difficult ones, right into the heart and soul of a listener.

March 1

Listen to understand. Do not respond or try to explain. Just listen and understand.

March 2

Getting your 'beauty sleep' has more to do with your attitude and emotional well-being than it does your looks. Although one who has a good attitude and is cheerful and happy is the most beautiful of all.

March 3

No one ever 'small talked' his way
into respect and standing.

March 4

It is true that sometimes our feelings
misinform us, but so do our
thoughts. Observe your feelings and
learn. Your feelings are not always
the enemy, nor are thoughts always
your ally. Ancient thinkers called the
balance between the two
'Tatramajjhattatā.'
It means 'equanimity.'

March 5

Equanimity is not remotely the same
thing as equality. Equanimity is quiet
dignity, a confident calmness
resulting from balance and
wellness. Equality is that
futile thing humans demand when
comparing themselves to others.

March 6

There are two types of rules. The first are the ones society needs all to obey for the safety and common good of the public. The second are those arbitrary and capricious rules some individuals imagine up to prevent others from 'playing in the neighborhood sandbox' or outperforming the established 'successful.' Obey the first and break the second.

March 7

Himalayan Sherpas greet
visitors with the term
'Tashi Deley,'
which means, 'I see,
recognize, and honor the
greatness within you.'

March 8

There is an ancient Hindi word,
'genshai,' that means 'never treat
someone in such a way that makes him
or her feel small, including
your own self.'

March 9

The founder of the stoic philosophy,
Zeno of Citium, said, 'Man conquers
the world by conquering himself.'
The African Swahilis have
their own philosophy, which
essentially says the
same thing. It is
'Jishinde Ushinde,'
which is translated,
'Conquer yourself to conquer.'

March 10

Peace is possible.
Why are we so afraid to listen?

March 11

Listening at first makes one feel
vulnerable to persuasion. However,
the fear of persuasion is irrational
because listening does not require
agreement. Listening is for
understanding.

March 12

When one refuses
to listen, he automatically
refuses to understand.

March 13

'The enemy is fear. We think it is hate, but it is really fear,' said Gandhi.
We are afraid to understand because we then see others are more like ourselves than not, and we feel vulnerable when we see ourselves in others.

March 14

Self-awareness is key to
everything. Without it, one is never
fully trusted. The unaware, and
narcissists, are siblings.
Those who lack self-awareness
are often the first to criticize others,
are the most vocal criticizers, and
often are the most worthy of
criticism themselves.

March 15

Do not fear being
influenced or persuaded
by those you do not
respect. You are listening
to understand, not
necessarily agreeing.

March 16

Listening to understand is not losing ground; you are gaining it. You may not respect them, but if you understand them, they will respect you. And if they respect you, the war will end.

March 17

'When Heaven is about to place a great responsibility on a man, it always first tests his resolution, exhausts his frame, and makes him suffer starvation and hardship, frustrates his efforts so as to shake him from his mental lassitude, toughen his nature and make good his deficiencies.'
–Mencius

March 18

In a world that has decided
that it's going to lose its mind,
be more kind my friends,
be more kind.'
–Frank Turner

March 19

Peace is possible, not through
'peace talks,' but through
'peace listening.'

March 20

It is going to take time, and
it is time I am willing to take. I
have to make time, and it is
time I am willing to make.

March 21

A 'great leader' is not truly ready
until he or she has suffered and
sorrowed equal to or greater than
those who will follow have
suffered and sorrowed.

March 22

Frequently, one side thinks the other is evil, so it resists. When one feels vulnerable, he resists. When one resists, he creates conflict. This is what Jesus meant when he said, 'Resist not evil.' Resist the urge to resist.

March 23

You know that person who always
leaves you feeling unwell? Angry,
aggravated, disrespected,
unsettled? Pay attention to those
feelings, but not that person.

March 24

While equality between humans is literally impossible and should not be entertained or encouraged because its very pursuit is undignified and unbecoming of the intelligent and reasoned, one should reject the presence of oppressive power disparity.

March 25

Seek understanding, seek answers, seek wisdom, seek a change of heart.

March 26

Can human nature be changed
Through reasoned persuasion?
Or can human nature only
Be changed through force?
Yet, the philosophical question seems futile
As neither seem to work well
And thus cannot be the answer.
There must be a third way
Such as, through some means
An elevation of humanity's view
Of what 'could and should be'
That will only work if individuals
Aspire to that view.
Therefore, human nature
Yields to 'aspiration of greatness.'

March 27

There is more beauty
Than there is ugly.
It is just that ugly is so loud.
Loud takes our attention
Away from the beautiful.
Do we remember that
Non-destructive power
Is quiet and gentle?
Loud makes us sad.
If I could I would
Make the world happy.
Happiness starts
With a whisper.

March 28

To know and understand someone
one must first know that person's
history and backstory,
what that person wants,
needs, hopes for,
aspires to, fears, causes of hurt,
what that person needs to feel safe,
and what makes that person
laugh and cry.
Only then can you say you
understand that person.

March 29

When someone tells you
How you made them feel,
Do not take it as an accusation.
Rather, welcome it as an invitation.

March 30

If you will learn to patiently watch,
You will have learned to patiently wait.

March 31

People want to help you.
Help them help you by being
precise in what you need.
If you need an English
muffin toasted dark
with extra butter and strawberry jam,
then make that explicitly clear.
If you help those who want to help you,
get right to the task.
You will find more and more
people willing to help you.

April 1

Be sweet, loving, kind,
helpful and respectful.

April 2

He 'saw' one
And it mattered
Then she 'saw' two
And it mattered more
Then they 'saw' a third
And eventually four
Oh, to be seen and heard!
Not ignored like before
Self-respect once shattered
Just grew and grew
Unlock a heart's prison door!
Let it begin anew!

April 3

In Latin,
'tranquilium'
means 'calmness.'
Tranquilium results
from observation.

April 4

'Contemplum' in Latin means 'a place for observation.' It is a place, set apart, carved out, made special, to think and meditate. The English derivative is 'contemplate.' Inherent in 'contemplum' is the Latin word 'templum.' It means 'temple' in English. A temple is a sacred place where one goes to observe and contemplate.

April 5

Thinking and feeling
are the best parts of being.

April 6

Crucifixion
Resurrection
He died for me and you!
Crucifixion
Resurrection
He Lives!
And we will too!

April 7

While listening to some
extraordinarily beautiful music
she said, 'I wish I could
make music like that.'
To which he responded,
'You make your own special
"music" in that unique way
that no one else can.
Keep making what you make,
as it is equally special and magical.'

April 8

The thing about great ideas
is that it takes great effort
to think about them.
Yet, these days
very few want to think
about anything important.

April 9

Of all the things
human beings
repeatedly do,
one reigns supreme
as that thing
humans do
particularly well:
Misunderstand each other.

April 10

There are two types of people:
Those who seek meaning
and those who hide from it.

April 11

The explanation
of 'everything'
is hiding in
plain sight.

April 12

Emotion gives everything meaning.
Only then does it begin to matter.
He who pretends to have little or none,
at least so seeming,
is the one on the verge of
emotional burst and shatter.

April 13

Do not become discouraged
while enduring suffering.
You are becoming
something special.

April 14

Have enough backbone
to put your foot down.
And enough courage to deal
with the fallout.

April 15

A ship is always
safe at the shore
But that is not what
it is built for.
                    —Albert Einstein

April 16

What our eyes 'evoke from
quanta' (Watts) on earth should not be
viewed as an anomaly within the
universe, but as a normality.
It is the universe expressing itself on
earth in the same manner it
expresses itself everywhere.
Therefore, what we observe on earth is
what also happens within
the universe generally.

April 17

Can human nature be changed
Through reasoned persuasion?
Or can human nature only
Be changed through force?
Yet, the philosophical
question seems futile
As neither seem to work well
And thus cannot be the answer
There must be a third way
Such as, through some means
An elevation of humanity's view
Of what 'could and should be'
That will only work if individuals
Aspire to that view.
Therefore, human nature
Yields to 'aspiration of greatness.'

April 18

An 'autoepistolary' is someone
who writes wise letters of
counsel, guidance and
encouragement to one's future self.

April 19

Sometimes staring up at the stars can
give you peace and clarity.
Sometimes it can be a distraction from
your goals and objectives. Make sure you
know which you are experiencing.

April 20

I have observed that human beings
interpret long periods of difficulty
such as isolation, illness, or financial
distress beyond one's control as
personal failure. It is a uniquely
human phenomena. It is irrational
and illogical, yet it even affects
some of the most rational and logical
individuals. One can sever
the illogical reaction to circumstances
beyond one's control
merely by curiously contemplating
why one thinks that way in the first
place. The antidote is found in
the subtle shift from
'feeling failure' to
'contemplative curiosity'
about why one feels failure
that does not exist.

April 21

There is an answer, a solution,
a resolution, a clarification,
closure, renewal, transition,
redemption, forgiveness, reconciliation,
accord, progression, reparation,
metamorphosis, harmony, grace,
mercy, remission, compassion,
and rebirth coming to you if you
welcome and receive it.

April 22

No matter how bad it gets
and how long it lasts,
you can and will defeat it.
You will pivot, adjust,
audible, observe, take note, and act.
You will defeat ugly with beauty.
You will defeat evil with virtue.
You will learn to bridle your tongue
and make your thoughts and emotions
heel to your higher self.
You were created to triumph.
And you will!

April 23

Rediscover the dignity
of personal responsibility.

April 24

People can feel, sense
and discern your quiet efforts
and sincere strivings.
Whether or not someone
verbally acknowledges
your efforts
is unimportant.
They know.

April 25

Here are the tools and skills that defeat the effects of adversity and trauma in real time:

Curious Observation

Watch it outside yourself like a movie

Curious Anticipation

Adversity carries with it the seeds of relief which appear subtly. Anticipate relief and then notice it when it manifests.
Anticipate beauty and goodness,
even if barely noticeable.

Record the Contrast

Write it down and tell the story of your heroic journey. Memorialize your unique perspective. Only when it is written down will your tragedy (caterpillar) become your triumph (butterfly).

Curiosity is the key!

April 26

Life can be crushing
when 'things happen' to you.
'Things' completely change
when 'you happen' to life!

April 27

Live and love it!

April 28

Choose one thing, simple
or great, to do today.
Then do it!
You will feel that special feeling of
accomplishment that humans
need to feel happy.
Do just one thing!

April 29

No matter how big
(or small) they see you,
remind them by your actions their view
of you is not big enough!

April 30

Repair of the human heart, mind
and soul comes with a
lifetime warranty.
Let it come!
Welcome and receive.

May 1

Kindness attracts kindness.
Happiness infects others.
Love conquers hate.

May 2

Do you know how significant
it is to hold another person's hand
when they want you to hold it?
There are a thousand things going
on in that simple moment.

May 3

It is extraordinary to
learn to love the mundane. That is
when all of the beauty hiding in plain
sight suddenly reveals itself.

May 4

Keep trying to find the words.
But don't worry if you can't.
The words will eventually find you.

May 5

If you are feeling down and having
a bad day and you want to feel better,
There is a simple solution;
Serve another.
Serving others helps you forget
your own woes and brings peace and
clarity to your problems.

May 6

Have you ever wondered why some people are afraid to act even when stunning success is likely, and others are afraid not to act even in the face of possible catastrophic failure?

May 7

Attempt not to communicate with
those who sleepwalk in circles.

May 8

It takes great courage to reduce what society insists is inevitable and unexplainable down to an ordinary question easily explainable by ordinary human beings.

May 9

Be very hesitant to accuse someone of wrongdoing even if you think you have ironclad proof. You could still be wrong. There is a powerful unseen force that protects the innocent.

May 10

There is a universal law that is
underutilized by humankind.
It is the 'Law of the Ask.'
One wonders why he never gets his fair
share. It could be that he never asks.

May 11

Duty becomes actionable on the
continuum between what one could do
for another, what one should do, and
what one must do.

May 12

One cannot be a "good man"
and ignore one's duty to help another.

May 13

Greatness must be affirmatively chosen. Do not confuse greatness with fame. The two are not the same. Although a few truly great people become famous, it is usually not the desire or choice of a great individual to be famous.

May 14

Put a stake in the ground and start fresh tomorrow. Keep swimming the same stroke through joy and sorrow. Everything will be alright.

May 15

Just because few men become great does not mean most men were incapable of becoming so. I reject the view that most men are incapable of great things or becoming great beings.

May 16

The effects of trauma are defeated in time
through choosing to be observationally curious
and observationally anticipatory.
One must first observe what is happening
around him or her and then choose to be curious
about it, leading to healthy exploration:
Actual or using one's imagination.
Then, one must observe, or remember, good
things he or she can anticipate.
A shower
A letter
A particular meal
Sleep
A good book, etc.
Anticipating 'simple things' without comparing
'great things' of the past neutralizes suffering
from trauma. Be observationally curious and
observationally anticipatory.

May 17

Just because one cannot explain it
does not mean it is unexplainable.

Just because one is a human being
does not automatically translate into
'being human.'

May 19

Some men will do 'anything'
and brag about it to 'everyone.'
Yet honorable men 'wherever'
refrain from doing 'some things,'
humbly bragging to 'no one,'
making them trustable in 'all things.'

May 20

No matter how good you are to other people and how much you are loved and respected, you will still be the villain in someone else's life story.

May 21

Mind your own business. Rumors are started when busybodies run out of gossip. Do not find yourself in the downstream flow of infected and contaminated talk. People gossip about those they think care.

May 22

Some quietly spend time
making a meaningful difference.
Many, many more
vociferously spend time creating the
perception that they are making a
meaningful difference.

May 23

The evil that one endures patiently
because it seems inevitable
becomes unbearable the moment
its elimination becomes conceivable.
—Alexis de Tocqueville

May 24

Hardship awakens virtue.
Virtue causes compatibility.
Compatibility yields confidence.
Confidence fosters valiance.
Valiance defeats hardship.

May 25

Only when there are things a man will
not do is he capable of doing great things.
This insight is nothing new.
Trustworthiness creates trust.

May 26

What one thinks and does affects others.
Even if one thinks it is none of
'their' business, bad behavior eventually
becomes everyone's business.

May 27

If someone trusts you,
that person has invested in you.
As with any investment,
what must you do?
Protect it from loss,
then help it grow too.

May 28

We belong here now.
We will belong there then.
Being is not who
or what you are.
It is 'that' you are.
Becoming is the process.
Being is the objective.

May 29

Freedom does not mean
A 'free for all.'
Freedom comes with
duties, obligations, ethics, and
moral obligations to one another.

May 30

The profound realization will occur when
you look back and see thousands of miles of
precisely threaded needles along the path.
Then you will know for sure.

May 31

Emerging virtue is as
unnoticeable as growing hair.

June 1

In the universe, there are
opposing forces locked in conflict.
Gravity opposes light.
Cold opposes heat.
Entropy opposes genesis.
Space opposes time.

June 2

Pay attention.
An amazing story is playing out
right in front of you.
It is called your life, and no one
can tell the story but you.

June 3

If you are still hurting from the
past, the past is your present.
If your present is your past,
your future is too.

June 4

One writes poetry
to let emotions out.
One reads poetry
to let emotions in.

June 5

Begin with a possible possibility.
Stick with it until it becomes a
definite possibility.
Persist in your determinations and
it will become a likelihood.
Unwavering belief coupled with
purposeful action turns a
likelihood into a certainty.

June 6

Why do you doubt who you are?
You are more important than a star.

June 7

Strive to be 'that' version of yourself today so when the future day arrives, that is who you are.

June 8

The teetering world is being
counterbalanced by a growing
magnitude of benevolents.

June 9

When you find your diamond, tell
others where to look for theirs.

June 10

Words are power.
By words, the universe, and a
flower. War or peace, explore or
cease. Life or death, twice the
depth. 'Word' is the substance of
'sword' with just an added 's.'

June 11

You see, an average person's life is REALLY complex and complicated. Not due to a single abstraction, but due to thousands.

June 12

Everything, and I mean everything, comes down to three things: Influence, Humility and Understanding. All human problems will be solved and resolved in due time by increasing all three.

June 13

Passing through the threshold of
self-delusion into self-awareness is a
terrifying thing until one experiences
the peace of mind there.

June 14

The most wonderful
and the most distressing
thing about being alive
is other people.

June 15

Choice is sovereign;
Consequence is too.

June 16

A truly impressive
outward demonstration
of inward strength
is quiet,
dignified waiting.

June 17

Do not be afraid
to write it down
because of what
might show up
on the paper.

June 18

'Actualized' means his ideas have become him, and he has become his ideas. An actualized mind aspires. A vulgar mind conspires.

June 19

I have observed that the problem with most men is that they lack aspiration, possess too much ambition, and do not understand the difference or why it matters. Emperor Aurelius said, 'A noble man compares and estimates himself by an idea which is higher than himself. The one produces aspiration. The other ambition. Accordingly, ambition must be an idea which is lower than its thinker, which is how a vulgar man aspires.'

June 20

What everyone really
wants to know
about themselves
is that they
will not just survive
but ultimately triumph.

June 21

The wise understand that
they understand little.

June 22

Do not ignore
the joy that is available
and waiting for you today.
I know it feels like
it has forsaken you,
but it never actually
left your side.

June 23

Worst times sometimes
follow best times.
Best times almost always
follow worst times.
Expect best times.

I walked through
the snow on that hot
summer day
and bobbed in the
dry riverbed
while the floods
washed me away.

June 25

The Grey Creek flows
and turns and creeps.
It stumbles and rolls
over a boulder that sleeps.
It shares its life;
its magnitude,
with those who need
its solitude.

June 26

Listen to the wind;
It talks.
Listen to the Silence;
It speaks.
Listen to your heart;
It knows.
–Native American Wisdom

June 27

Wise people say,
'Please elaborate.'
'Tell me more.'
'I want to understand.'
'Help me understand.'
'Thank you for sharing.'

June 28

Ask yourself this:
Are you damaged?
Or are you polished?
All of those collisions
you have experienced
counterintuitively
have not damaged you
but have polished you
into a bright sheen.
Perhaps you simply
need new glasses.

June 29

You are beautiful.
You are important.
You matter to humanity.
People care about you.
I care about you.
You make a difference.
You matter to me.
I thank you sincerely.

June 30

It is not the mountain that moves.
It is you.

July 1

The America of today, if truth be told,
is in no worse shape than she was ten, twenty,
or even one hundred years ago. She is stronger
and actually improving. Here is why: We nearly
lost the Revolutionary War on at least two
separate occasions were it not for rogue
winter storms that wrecked the Redcoats'
visibility in one instance and drove back their
boats and warships in another.
The Civil War was also nearly lost but for the
Confederacy having misplaced its battle plans
and strategic documents in an abandoned tent,
later to be found by a Union scout.

July 2

Want to remain free? Never forget the two 'tens:' The Ten Commandments and the Ten Amendments. Together, 'Liberty's Twenty.'

July 3

A nation is great when its
citizens are good.
America's citizens have always
been good, which is why
America has always been great.

July 4

I pledge allegiance
to the Flag of the
United States of America,
and to the Republic for which it stands,
one Nation under God,
indivisible,
with liberty and justice for all.

July 5

Each individual American must have enough courage to present his or her idea or complaint in the public square: To lay it bare to criticism, to test it, to prove it, and respectfully accept its rejection and defeat if it comes to that. If accepted, graciously give it as your gift to society. If you have an idea, have the courage to bring it forth and let the people decide whether it is good for all.

July 6

The colonists must have been
astonished beyond measure
with the development
and implementation of the
Declaration of Independence,
Constitution, and other supporting
documents. To them it must have seemed
like a miracle, and it was. America must
recapture that awe and wonder.

July 7

If you want to enjoy the privilege of
American citizenship, other Americans
expect you to understand and obey two self-
existing, self-evident, universal laws. The
first is to 'do all you have agreed to do.'
Keep your word. Keep your promises. Don't
break your contracts, etc. The second is 'do
not encroach on the person or property of
another individual.' As Americans, we
implicitly agree to the second. If we do all
we have agreed to do, then we by definition
should not encroach on others.
'Encroachment' can mean anything from
talking or laughing too loud, thereby
interfering with other conversations
happening around us, driving while
intoxicated and crashing into another
person's vehicle, all the way on the other
spectrum of murder.

'Encroachment' includes anything that interferes with another person's life, liberty, or the pursuit of their happiness. It does not include being 'offended' because another person pursues his or her happiness differently than you do. Excluding pettiness, encroachment takes many forms, and it is neither welcome nor accepted in the American way. If everyone in American society would obey those two simple laws that are capacitated to be followable by virtually everyone, there would be peace and harmony in homes and in public. Prisons would be empty.

July 8

These events are not luck.
They are caused by a Being, more
intelligent than and superior to us.
We then conclude that this
Supremely Intelligent and Benevolent
Being wants America to exist
and go on existing.

July 9

History has shown us, time and time again, that America's people are a diverse and complicated bunch. We are a multi-talented tapestry of enormous untapped potential, quietly surging, nearly glowing as we bend and sway against the political and economic wind gusts of the day.

July 10

Our Founding Fathers were
great men. Very few men today
can even scratch the surface of the
depth of their character,
bravery, and moral excellence.

July 11

'There is not a man living who wishes more sincerely than I do to see a plan adopted for the abolishment of slavery.'

–George Washington to Robert Moore, 1786

July 12

'I am in prison. I cannot imagine in
my current state what liberty will feel
like. Liberation from prison will
probably feel similar to what the
colonists felt when the war ended.'
–Matthew D. Hutcheson

July 13

'If America is not great, then
what nation is? If America's
citizens are not good, then what
nation's citizens are?'
—Matthew D. Hutcheson

July 14

As Martin Luther King, Jr. so eloquently said, as applied to the nations of the earth and its citizens, 'Each [Nation] has two selves, and the great burden of [a nation's] life is to always try to keep that higher self in command. Don't let the lower self take over.' If [America's] 'higher self' is good, then America will be great. America's 'higher self' has always been in command; America has always been great.

July 15

Socialism
is communism's little brother.

Communism
first excites, then confuses, then destroys.

Capitalism
is naturally occurring.

July 16

Just because few men become great does not mean most men were incapable of becoming so.

July 17

Only when there are things a
man will not do is he capable
of doing great things.

July 18

Want to know who you really are? Choose what is right in the moment you desperately want something that is wrong.

July 19

Great 'thinking leaders' bring
about change through
benevolence.

July 20

Let not the actions or words of
others determine your direction.
With YOUR mind and heart as
YOUR source, resolutely find and
chart YOUR course.

July 21

Sustained and persistent
courage is possible only by
being morally in the right.

July 22

What makes life fair is that it is
unfair to everyone. Relish in it.

July 23

"Waste no more time arguing
about what a good man should be.
Be one."
— Marcus Aurelius

July 24

Some men talk about what
they should do. Great men do
what they should do.

July 25

Leaders must strengthen the state
politically, economically and morally.
Moral leadership is the more
important of the three.

July 26

"Fear begets anger.
Anger begets hate.
Hate begets suffering."
—Aikido Center of Los Angeles

July 27

Conflict is not about our differences.
It is about a fear of our differences.

July 28

Go out of your way to do what
needs to be done. You know.

July 29

If it is true that history repeats itself, then it is a plausible hypothesis that some (or perhaps all) of the historical scenarios will occur again in our immediate or long-term future.

July 30

Capitalism
You own your capital and control your life.

Socialism
The state controls your capital and your life.

Communism
The state OWNS you and all capital.

July 31

America's destiny has been absolutely littered by an almost bizarre series of impossibly close calls, extending far beyond those of our Revolutionary and Civil Wars. Further examples include the United States' narrowly winning the race against Germany to construct World War II's first atomic bomb—and in the 11th hour to break the enigma code.

August 1

Anciently, Aristotle called VIRTUE the 'mean between the extremes.' It means the point of balance in one's life. Later, beginning around the 1600s, philosophers began to define VIRTUE as 'excellence.' Being a virtuous person means being an excellent person.

August 2

Virtue manifests in our characters like
fruit ripening on a tree.
Virtue ripens within us as a result of
life's extreme difficulties.
Life's ups and downs are called
'vicissitudes.' Vicissitude makes virtue.

August 3

A human being cannot become an excellent person without repeatedly experiencing extreme difficulty. And to be compatible with our future Heavenly home, we must be an excellent person, and that takes time and difficulty.

August 4

No difficulty is wasted. No difficulty is
unfair. No difficulty is meaningless.
Difficulty, or vicissitude, life's
ups and downs and tragedies, causes
excellence to develop within us.

August 5

What is a skill-trait? It is a hybrid of developed skills that can be learned, practiced, and used to make life easier, coupled with the development of excellent personal traits of character through vicissitude.

August 6

Choose curiosity in every
adversity as opposed to anxiety.

Choose anticipation of good to
come as opposed to impatience.

Choose a good attitude as
opposed to bitterness.

Choose virtue by being faithful in every
particular as opposed to giving up.

August 7

Curiosity defeats fear.
Anticipation defeats dread.
Good attitude defeats bitterness.
Virtue defeats surrender.

August 8

Trust is not something that suddenly
exists after a single, big event.
Rather, it is the accumulation of
seemingly insignificant, small events.

August 9

Virtue is like 'rhodium' in your character. Once virtue is gained, it must not be lost. Think of it as a precious investment you have made in yourself. Giving up would cause such a loss, so virtue defeats surrender. (Rhodium is the most valuable metal and exists within the platinum group of metals. Palladium is the second most valuable of the precious metals and exists within the platinum group. Gold, the one you thought was the most valuable, is currently the third most valuable metal.)

Source: Impress Jewelry Creations

August 10

The wise anchor to wisdom,
fools anchor to foolishness, and
neither are willing to move.

August 11

When one has been under pressure
for so long, a diamond is sure to
be in there somewhere.
One only need recognize it.

August 12

The time will come when good manners, graciousness, well-spokenness, approachability, reasonableness, and a good demeanor will be valued above all due to scarcity and demand.

August 13

There is not triumph in avoidance.
It is going to hurt. No question
about it. Don't hide or cower. Face
it down and walk through it.
Triumph awaits on the other side.

August 14

Walks, flowers and handwritten
notes to others are smart. Each is
a way to spark joy into your heart.

August 15

It is going to take a leader with
skills never before needed,
understanding never before attained,
and trust never before gained.

August 16

The ones who say you can't are really just afraid you will.

August 17

Don't let others' opinions frame
what you do in life. If you like to
run, then run . . . even if someone
says you aren't shaped like a runner
or look like a runner. The same
applies to anything in life.

August 18

The key to permanent, deep, rich, safe and fulfilling relationships is vulnerability. Vulnerability in this context is not weakness or willingness to be exploited or abused. Rather, it is trusting that a pain, fear, sorrow, flaw, mistake, regret, feeling, hope, dream, aspiration, success (while knowing you could be crushed by the response or reaction) will be tenderly received into the heart of the other.

August 19

Mind your own business. Remember, rumors are started when busybodies run out of gossip. Do not find yourself in the downstream flow of infected and contaminated talk. People gossip about those they think it bothers.

August 20

Your story will save someone
else in the future, so write it down.
Right now, even though you don't
know it, you are someone's hero.
Do not let him or her down.

August 21

One of humanity's
Supreme paradoxes
Is this . . .
If one wants
To be 'big'
One must first learn
To be 'small'

August 22

Plato said,
'The greatest wealth
is to be content
with a little wealth.'
I say, 'The greatest wisdom
is to be discontent
with a little wisdom.'

August 23

We each have full control over
what will, and what will not,
become our life's regrets.

August 24

You and I may not agree on what beauty is. That is the beauty of life.

August 25

Linger not in echo chambers, nor
let thy voice 'echo' therein.

August 26

I am impressed by thoughts.
Your thoughts, their thoughts.
Things I've learned and things I've taught.
I prefer mind-bending more than not.
Thoughts that make me wonder.
Thoughts that tear my brain asunder.
Ideas that make me ponder.
Philosophical, scientific, and mystery-history.
Intellectual poetry.
Esoteric knowetry.
Gossip and petty complaints disgust me.
I loathe what small talk pretends to be.
Don't talk about you, and
I won't talk about me.
Don't tell me about things you bought
Because I don't care.
Just tell me things you thought
And you'll have my attention to spare.

August 27

Yet man
is born
unto trouble,
as the
sparks fly
upward.
　　　–Job 5:7

August 28

It is true
that children need
parental guidance.
After which,
parental trust
must immediately
follow.

August 29

Seemingly impossible things to
explain can be explained.
However, the 'explanation of everything'
is not an 'explanation for everyone.'

August 30

Sages speak when there is
something important to say.
Fools speak because they just
always have to say something.

August 31

Enjoy the harvest;
It is a gift from God.
Reap what you sow,
In life and in what you grow.

September 1

It is who I am that matters,
not where I am.
Why all the clatter?

September 2

There is a fine line
between a numerator
and a denominator.
Only a fraction
will understand.

September 3

Increasing trust,
diminishing suspicion.
Increasing suspicion,
diminishing trust.

September 4

Trust is simple.
Distrust is complex.

September 5

No matter how
trustworthy you may
actually be,
there will always
be someone who does
not trust you.
They do not have to.
And not everyone
deserves your trust, either.

September 6

Teach children correct principles
and live by those principles so
adults' contradictions do not
become the children's.

September 7

I do not need to be right,
and you should not need
me to be wrong.

September 8

'I am HERE FOR you'
means:
'Think well of me for saying it,
but please don't ask me to
actually do something for you.'

In contrast,
'I am FOR you'
means:
'I am your ally,
and your advocate.'
That REALLY means something.

September 9

Don't push,
Encourage.
Don't urge,
Inspire.
Don't reprove,
Teach.

September 10

The first words
spoken by a person
are like a selfie
of a deeper sort.

September 11

Remember that a little is a lot.
Be grateful for what you've got.
Don't be someone you're not.
What they think ain't squat.
You can and you will,
never cannot.
Always take the shot,
be Johnny-on-the-spot.
That negative thought? Swat.
Congratulations!
You found what you sought.

September 12

If you are a good memory for
others, you have succeeded
brilliantly.

September 13

What is the purpose
of purpose? The purpose of my
purpose is you.

September 14

You regret not doing it then.
Do not regret not doing it now.
Remember what made you proud
yesterday. Choose something to
make you proud tomorrow.

September 15

Society has been indoctrinated to recycle everything: plastics, paper, metal, and, of course, recycling is good and wise. However, it is the unintended effects that society labors under now. 'Recycling' has seeped into our subconscious, and we now recycle everything. Our bad day. Those mean words. Hurts from years ago. Misunderstandings from yesterday. Anxiety is caused by recycling garbage in one's head.

September 16

The character of your friends
will be revealed by the slightest
petty misunderstanding or
miscommunication.

September 17

There is something fundamentally wrong with inviting someone to leave his or her comfort zone to 'sit at your table.' While intended to 'seem' inclusive, if you really mean it, why don't you ask someone if you can leave YOUR comfort zone and sit at theirs?

September 18

'When God wants to send you
a gift, He wraps it up in a problem.
And the bigger the gift that God
sends you, the bigger the problem.'
       –Dr. Norman Vincent Peale

September 19

The marble
statue of you
is almost ready
for revealing.

September 20

Here's a little secret:
You do not have to be chronically sad,
anxious, angry, unhappy, defeated, or
disappointed. If you really want to, you
can drop all of that in the bucket right
now and celebrate.

September 21

Society's greatest
problem is that
those 'who know'
stopped teaching
'those who don't.'

September 22

A possibility
is a hint from God.
One must follow it.
—Soren Kierkegaard

September 23

'If you're so smart,' says one person to another, 'why do you need a dictionary?' To which the second person replied, 'If I am as smart as you say, it is because I use the dictionary.'

September 24

Keep the knowledge,
remember the experience,
untether the pain,
and start again.

September 25

YOU matter!
YOU matter to some, and
YOU matter to me.
If YOU matter one,
YOU matter to three.
YOU matter to them,
YOU matter to ten!
Never forget who YOU've got.
Truly, YOU matter a lot!

September 26

Prison helped me see and understand
the hidden, invisible, silent,
incomprehensible, and unthinkable.
My dimensions are forever altered.

September 27

I find it peculiar
that you find it odd that
what I hold is frozen and
what you hold is thawed.

September 28

When you are reeling from it, you are feeling it. When you are feeling it, you are revealing it. When you are revealing it, you are not concealing it. By not concealing it, you are healing it.

September 29

There is a reason 'small talk' leaves others feeling unsettled. It makes others feel subtly manipulated and feeling 'small.'

September 30

Stop small talk
Big talk
Brag talk
Sad talk
Gossip talk
Flattery and
Endless drivel talk
Be thoughtful and
Reserved in your words
Be precise in what you say
Ask politely for what you need
And be gracious with
your noes and yeses
Then watch how things
Begin to change
For you

October 1

Refinement Progression
=
Aggression
Assertion
Ambition
Aspiration
Actualization

October 2

You and I are, respectively, one
half of another person's 'wheel.'
Therefore, it is imperative that we
bring balance to the rotations of
that wheel. Never, ever should we
be the cause of imbalance in
another person's rotations.

The reason philosophy is so important is because it trains the human mind to efficiently sift the valuable ideas from those that are worthless.

October 4

Everything is too loud, too noisy, too busy. Life is meant to be quiet; smell the flowers, savor the peach, preserve the harvest, laugh with the children, sing to the baby, cuddle the kitty, feed the bunnies.

October 5

Be calm today. Be deliberate and intentional. Get up and get moving. Calculate. Decide. Act. Be precise. Clean yourself up. Clean up your act. Smile with your eyes. Those are today's marching orders.

October 6

It is time to belong.
Not merely for a time,
but for all time.

October 7

Although belonging be absent for
thee, as far as the eye can see.
When belonging can be found in
no other place on land or on sea,
come, my friend, you may
belong with me.

October 8

If you want to feel like royalty,
be kind.
If you want others to feel like royalty,
serve them.

October 9

Human words were never meant
to fully describe human
experience. Only emotion and
reason are capable of
filling the gap.

October 10

Families of prisoners exert heroic efforts so there is something for the prisoner to come home to. The prisoners exert heroic efforts so they can just make it home. It takes both to survive this or any horrific experience.

October 11

Document your experiences and
express your achievements.
Vulnerability is power.

October 12

Invert and normalize your
distresses. Then, unexpected
eases will result in unexpected
joys. This is what I call the
'philosophy of invertibility.'

October 13

There are four diminishing
measures of wisdom. First, a full
measure of wisdom is the ability
to see the consequence of an
action not yet taken.

October 14

Second, a lesser measure of
wisdom on the downward sloping
continuum is the ability to see and
feel the consequence of an errant
action just taken.

October 15

Third, lesser still, the ability
and willingness to correct
the errant action.

October 16

Fourth, the lowest form of
wisdom is finally understanding
the mistake of failing to see, feel,
and correct a previous mistake.

October 17

As Confucius explained, 'If you
make a mistake and do not
correct it, this is called a mistake.'
What remains after the fourth and
lowest measure of wisdom is
essentially the animal instinct
articulated by Will Rogers. 'When
you find yourself in a hole, stop
DIGGING.' That, essentially, is
the entire spectrum of wisdom.

October 18

VINCIT QUI SE VINCIT.
'He Conquers Who Conquers Himself.'
–Ancient Roman saying

October 19

Wisdom is a curious mix of
contemplation and emotion.
Therefore, a fulness of
wisdom requires both
thoughtfulness and empathy.

October 20

Logic dictates there must be an
actor: a doer, a knower, of all
things, because all things are
knowable. Also, because we can
observe 'spooky action
at a distance (Einstein).' There is
a Supreme actor, doer, knower.

October 21

What can we infer about the existence of a 'Supreme-Intelligence-Actor-Knower?' Logic demands that if there is a lesser intelligence, there must be a greater.

October 22

During a storm on the ocean, remain in
the boat and trust the captain.
If you jump out, you will drown.
Whereas if you stay in the boat, you
will probably get seasick and
dehydrated, but you will survive.

October 23

Set up future consequences.
If you are wise, and understand,
you will set up good consequences.

October 24

At this very moment there is at least
one person in your circle who is
rightfully awe-inspired by your courage,
resilience and determination.

October 25

One can experience chaos
without becoming chaos.

October 26

A cold heart
is a wounded heart.
A hard heart
is an angry heart.
A closed heart
is a betrayed heart.
A distant heart
is a sad heart.

October 27

Water spends some time on the
mountain peak as ice;
in the low valley as a stream;
in the vast sea drifting around in
currents it cannot control;
and in the air as vapor.
Human beings are much the same:
high, low, cold, hot, drifting, floating.
But sometimes we are in a glass
that another drinks to survive.

October 28

Setting a good example usually
requires a multi-decade commitment.

October 29

Talk is cheap due to maximum supply
and minimum demand.

October 30

That some do not 'see' does not
mean others do not. That others
do not presently 'see' does not
mean they are incapable of 'seeing'
in the future. That others are able
to 'see' now does not mean they
will always 'see' then. 'Vision' is
enabled by rightness of heart.

October 31

A wise person resolves to be primarily silent. Why? The simpleton will not understand. The indifferent will diminish. The uninitiated will defile. The malicious will distort. The unwise will misconstrue. The imprudent will run, trip, and fall upon words that are sharper than scissors. That leaves 'speaking' to other wise ones who likewise wish to be silent.

November 1

One of the most exciting things about
life is that 'life' is going to happen
to each of us no matter what, and we have
little or no heads-up of how or where it is
going to happen. So, 'life' is one big
element of surprise. For those who learn to
be curious (not anxious) and anticipatory
(not impatient), life will be wonderful, even
when really bad things happen. One of life's
great mysteries is that we can be happy
amid adversity and suffering. We will
elaborate more upon that later.

November 2

Thank you for your courage.
Courage, in my opinion, is one
of the greatest virtues.

November 3

God is not willing to do
everything, and thus take away
our free will and that share of
glory which belongs to us.

November 4

It is said that 'by their fruits you shall know them,' meaning that the RESULTS in the lives of followers of Jesus Christ will be superior to the results in the lives of those who don't. But for fruit to be borne, there must be opposition, resistance, tribulation, and adversity. Otherwise, the virtues needed for perfection will not be awakened or coaxed out of hiding.

November 5

At that moment, it will seem like 'a conclusion' to the journey will never arrive. But it will, and eventually does. Until then, one must continue forward, 'swimming the same stroke,' day after day until it does.

November 6

Courage, grit, persistence, endurance, etc., are all naturally renewable resources within you. You will see. But you will have to dig deep within and that will carry you beyond the limits of your currently known reserve of courage, where, ironically, you will discover more.

November 7

Sometimes a 'twisted life' is
twisted just enough to see clearly.
—Marcy Nichols Pooler

November 8

As Johann Wolfgang von Goethe so eloquently put it, 'In the realm of ideas everything depends on enthusiasm . . . in the real world all rests on perseverance.' Digging deep into mysterious reserves within is something I understand well. At that moment, it seems like 'a conclusion' to a journey will never arrive. But it will, and eventually does. Until then, one must continue forward, 'swimming the same stroke,' day after day until it does. Every step into that dark place where everything within you screams 'stop and collapse' creates a foundation of strength that will never fade away and can always be drawn upon in the future.

November 9

You are moving forward, sailing
into a sea of uncertainty, knowing
that the ocean will only grow
more turbulent as you go.
Enjoy the journey.
Respect the difficulties.
Celebrate the triumph.
Pray in gratitude when it's over.

November 10

Do not be afraid of the future.
There is purpose in ups and downs.
There is great reason to hope and dream.
Do not ever give up.
Do not dread.
Do not fear.
It's just for a season, after all.

November 11

Don't reprove.
Teach.

November 12

'Doing' is important for happiness.
Even more importantly, 'gratitude' for the
privilege 'to do' is the universal key to the
'master lock.' Beginning to see? Let's talk.

November 13

Things happen within the rhythm and pace of nature. When one slows down and intentionally synchronizes with that rhythm, nature begins cooperating.

November 14

Trees are not dormant. They live in a continual life cycle of blossoming, to new leaves, to letting the leaves fall for a period of rest, to allow the new blossoms to grow again in the spring. The tree knows that this cycle must happen in order to reach its full potential. Are we not unlike the tree? We too must continually shed old ideas, habits, and attitudes to allow new, better growth into our lives. Every season is important to reach our full potential.

November 15

I love flowers, 78-degree days, tropical fruit, baby animals, stream fishing, alone time, meekness, my family, big talk (as opposed to small talk), intimacy, vulnerability, art, philosophy, ally-relationships, and most of all, my Father in Heaven who shows me endless mercies and tender kindnesses.

November 16

To live happily, learn to LIKE
the ones you LOVE.

November 17

There is a reason the story of Joseph in Egypt is so important. It is a personal reminder to each of us that we are always on Heavenly Father's mind and that He is always planning for our ultimate triumph if in our hearts that is truly what we want Him to do for us.

November 18

Life is like being stuck between
two pieces of coarse sandpaper.
The smoother we become, the finer
the sandpaper becomes, until
we are perfectly polished and the
sandpaper is a soft hammock lightly
cradling us as we gently sway. The key
is to not fight the polishing.

November 19

Given what you have experienced, your feelings
are normal and natural. Breathe and cry your way
through it. It's going to hurt for a while. I am
FOR you. Commune with others you know for
certain are also FOR you. But understand that
emotional pain has a diminishing shelf life. Pain
begins to diminish immediately and will
eventually level out so there is just enough 'hurt'
to help you remember, but not so much as to
prolong your suffering. Do not fight this process.
Let it hurt and let it slowly subside naturally. Just
remember to breathe and cry your way through
it. You are so brave. You are okay now, and you
will be okay then.

November 20

The beginning of understanding is understanding that one lacks understanding. The beginning of wisdom begins when one who thinks he is 'big' suddenly understands he has always been 'small.' Only when one finally understands he is 'unwise' and 'small' will his 'wise-size' change from 'small' to 'tall.'

November 21

Tacet qui scit . . .
'He who knows is silent.'

November 22

Feeling grateful seals shut the
portal to feeling hateful.
The two cannot coexist.

November 23

Most of the people within each of our respective circles have something to say and need someone safe to say it to. They need someone to listen to them right now.

November 24

I said you look beautiful because you are beautiful. Those who think they are not are the most beautiful of all.

November 25

The highest security prisons are not surrounded by razor wire and guards. Rather, such prisons are human minds lacking vision, imagination, curiosity, anticipation, insight, understanding, hope, and perseverance coupled with the inability and/or refusal to memorialize thoughts and experiences. Liberation begins with truthfully writing and reflecting upon one's own story.

November 26

Those who are truly wise can 'see the consequence of an action not yet taken.' And, if a consequence can be seen in advance, it can be chosen if good or avoided if bad. Thus, the wise, by and large, consciously choose their consequences. The unwise do not understand that they, too, are choosing their consequences, albeit unconsciously. Imagine how different the average person's life would be if he or she also chose consequences consciously.

November 27

The modern concept of 'zen' is not a religious one. It is philosophical. It means 'contemplation upon the nature of things.' Thus, philosophically speaking, a 'zen zone' is that attained place within a person where everything feels balanced and harmonious.

November 28

To introduce yourself to yourself, you must embark on the long and unspeakably painful journey on the crucible train through the land of seemingly never-ending and never-yielding tribulation.

November 29

Let yourself like yourself. Let yourself see your goodness. Stop fueling the 'anti-you' division and conflict within yourself.

November 30

To say, 'I like you,' may have deeper
meaning within a context than
saying 'I love you.' Many people
'love' those they do not 'like.' But
actually liking the ones you love is a
rare gift and a treasure.

December 1

To experience these astonishing
results in one's life, he or she must
be faithful in every particular to the
Savior and in living His Gospel.

December 2

Never forget that you are a child
of Almighty Supremacy. He has
planted some of His powers within
you, and those powers will not let you
down so long as you cling to Him
in all things, and in every particular.
You have the power to overcome.
You will overcome.

December 3

To be one's best,
prayer is the test.
A prayer is what you should say
when you don't want to pray.

December 4

Just because our relationship with
Heavenly Father and Jesus
is 'personal' does not mean
it should not also be 'formal.'
Pray with reverence and respect to
our Father in the name of His Son
who holds all creation in His hands.
Never forget THEY are
your biggest fans.

December 5

In the beginning, God said, "Let there be light." That statement is not an invitation. It is a solemn decree.

December 6

Humpty Dumpty sat on a wall,
Humpty Dumpty had a great fall.
All the King's horses
And all the King's men
Couldn't put Humpty
together again . . .
BUT THE KING COULD!

Jesus Christ is our KING. He not only is
putting Humpty (all of us) back together
again, He will succeed in perfecting all
those who will not push Him away. It is
THE PERFECTION DECREE.

December 7

When you see your virtues tested, survive
and ultimately bear fruit, you will know
that it is HE who does it for you.

And by HIS fruits ye shall know HIM.

December 8

Feast upon the scriptures until
'you are what you eat.'

Making scriptures a part of you
is such an amazing treat.

Accompanied by truth as you
walk from place to place.

Whenever you need them,
you'll have them, just in case.

December 9

A rare and admirable quality in a person is the ability to simultaneously hold multiple conflicting, opposing, or contradictory ideas, views, concepts, and/or beliefs simultaneously in his or her mind; each 'thought' being worthy of consideration in its own right and degree; each leading to varying inversely-correlated conclusions; each likely at odds with the other 'thoughts;' each seeming to possess (at least initially) potentially more or less equal value or truth.

December 10

Choice is sovereign.
Consequence is too.

December 11

He knows you,
and I think
you know Him too.

December 12

For Him to make one perfect, He must activate, actualize, and perfect every virtue within him or her. Virtues, ironically, do not activate themselves. Virtues must be awakened from a deep sleep. Other virtues must be coaxed out of hiding. The awakening and coaxing occur in the hot crucible of tribulation and adversity. There is no other way. God knows that. Deep down, we know that too. Pain and suffering are necessary to activate, actualize, and perfect every virtue.

December 13

The Savior, through His gospel, is trying to teach us how we can defeat every adversity by being faithful in every particular. That is how it is done.

When we are faithful in every particular, fear begins to subside, and we become curious about a real or perceived situation or event instead of being terrified by it.

When we are faithful in every particular, we become filled with anticipation for what good event might happen next instead of being filled with dread about what bad event might happen instead.

When we are faithful in every particular, our attitude towards life improves to the point where bitterness does not take hold.

When we are faithful in every particular, our virtues blossom in adversity, and any temptation to surrender, or give up, is defeated by the developing 'excellence of person' within us.

December 14

Faith is belief in action
Faith begins with tiny pursuits
All you need is a tiny fraction
To activate your boots
Faith only seeks
That which is true
Faith scales Supernal peaks
And is something that you do
Ultimately you will see
It is not the
Mountain that moves
It is you

December 15

The test of a spiritual philosophy,
method, doctrine, creed, religion, or
ethos is whether its concept of Deity is
glorified and exalted in proportion to, or
instead inversely to, humankind. For
example, does a Deity glorify itself by
elevating, or by minimizing, its
creations? Is God great because
humans are not? Or is God's greatness
inversely correlated with human
ungreatness? Alternatively, is God great
because He will make humans
proportionately great if we will let Him?
I cannot believe in the former, but
unabashedly embrace the latter.

December 16

Are you capable of seeing and acknowledging virtues or glimmers of light in people you otherwise believe to be evil? That capability reveals an advanced benevolent character.

December 17

It all begins with
WONDER
then
CONTEMPLATION
then a
QUESTION
then an
ANSWER
then
ACTION
then
WONDER

December 18

The phrase A THRILL OF HOPE from a favorite Christmas carol is worth contemplation. How can we have hope when the future is so uncertain? Do I feel a THRILL OF HOPE in today, tomorrow, next year, the eternities? You can feel the thrill. Feel it because you know that any circumstance that we are in–good or bad–is temporary. Have hope that you will live again with our Father and his Son, our Savior, Jesus Christ. It is okay to get down and discouraged. The Thrill of Hope will bring you back. I hope these words bring you a thrill as you contemplate your hope in your life.

December 19

I hope you sit and enjoy the glow of
the Christmas tree lights this year.
The lights will not glow without
proper power. We too will glow
when we allow the proper power into
our lives. Only the Savior, Jesus
Christ, can properly power us to glow
to our full potential. Sit and enjoy
the glow of the Christmas lights. Sit
and enjoy your own glow as well.

December 20

The key is to
L I V E L I F E
with all your heart and soul.
Wherever you may be and
wherever you may go.

December 21

Excitement and anticipation
for what comes next is a gift of
curiosity. It is a beautiful little thing,
and it is the sibling of hope.

December 22

The Old Testament (Amos 8:11) says people will stagger from sea to sea and wander from north to east, searching for the word of the Lord. Why not 'north to south?'

It is because the South has little or no profound spiritual or symbolic meaning to humanity. On the other hand, the region or culture we call the 'East' possesses deep and rich meaning.

Thus, from 'north to east' truly suggests something profound for humanity to contemplate upon.

For millennia, 'East' symbolized spiritual awakening, fresh beginnings, the assurance we can always 'rise' tomorrow (like the sun) and move to a higher level of awareness and spiritual wisdom as life progresses.

The Bible says, 'Wise men' came from the 'East.'

December 23

The Savior of the World was born in the springtime. Flocks in the field need grass to eat. Shepherds do not sleep with their flocks at night in the dead of winter. Ja'far al-Sadiq (the sixth Imam) correctly said Christ was born near the time of the Spring Equinox. Modern revelation pinpoints the date as April 6th.

December 24

Darkness of Sheol is gone
Lightness of soul has won
He was the Christ Child
So meek and so mild
We must be like Him
Sing out the Christmas hymn

December 25

December 25 marks an important day following the winter solstice when light begins to exceed darkness; highly symbolic of the 'Light of the World's' entrance into and darkness's loosening grip upon. For this reason, we celebrate Christmas on December 25, and it is perfectly fine that we do.

December 26

DEFEND
the weak and the fatherless
UPHOLD
the cause of the poor
and the oppressed
RESCUE
the weak and the needy
DELIVER
them from the
hands of the wicked

December 27

Take the good
Memories of the past
And make them
Present again

December 28

When I looked
I felt it
In my soul
Some stranger's
Inspiration made
Me whole

December 29

Everything experienced up 'til now
is merely rudimentary. Wait 'til you
see what comes next.

December 30

Write your future self a letter
today. What will it say?

December 31

Let next year come in happily.
It begins with you and me.
Let peace prevail.
Let kind words sail.
Soft hearts feel light.
A smile, so right.
One need not do much.
Just the human touch.
Goodbye sadness, goodbye storm,
hello gladness, joy is born.

Other books to enjoy by
MATTHEW D. HUTCHESON

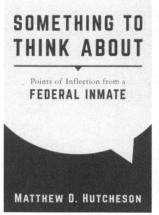